TIGER
WOODS

TIGER
WOODS

CARL EMERSON
THE CHILD'S WORLD®, INC.

ON THE COVER...

Front cover: Tiger smiles as he holds up the trophy from the 1999 PGA Championship.
Page 2: Tiger watches his ball sail down the fairway at the 2000 Nissan Open.

Library of Congress Cataloging-in-Publication Data
Emerson, Carl.
Tiger Woods / by Carl Emerson.
p. cm.
Includes index.
ISBN 1-56766-833-X (alk. paper)
1. Woods, Tiger—Juvenile literature.
2. Golfers—United States—Biography—Juvenile literature.
3. Racially mixed people—United States—Biography—Juvenile literature.
[1. Woods, Tiger. Golfers. 3. Racially mixed people—Biography.]   I. Title.
GV964.W66 E64 2000
796.352'092—dc21
00-038340

PHOTO CREDITS

© AP/Wide World Photos: 6, 10, 13, 15, 16, 19, 22
© Michael Zito/SportsChrome-USA: 2, 20
© Rob Tringali, Jr./SportsChrome-USA: cover
© SportsChrome-USA: 9

TABLE OF CONTENTS

A SPECIAL CHAMPION

Tiger Woods stood over a putt he knew would make history. He was on the 18th green at Augusta National, and he was about to win the prestigious Masters **tournament.** Leading the tournament by 12 shots, he already knew he was going to win. But this putt was still important to Tiger.

If he made it, we would set a new record for the lowest score ever in the Masters. Tiger's lifelong goal was to be the best golfer ever. This putt would be another step toward reaching that goal.

Making history at Augusta National meant more to Tiger than it might to other golfers. There was a time when only white people were allowed to play on this **course.** Now Tiger, who is of mixed heritage but is mostly African American, was going to be its champion.

Tiger stroked the putt, and as it rolled into the hole, the crowd erupted and Tiger pumped his fist. As he walked off the green a record-setting champion, Tiger hugged his father Earl, and they both sobbed. Their dreams were coming true.

Tiger celebrates as he leaves the 18th green after winning the 1997 Masters.

A PRODIGY

Tiger Woods showed signs of being a golf superstar very early in his life. He was born on December 30, 1975. His real name is Eldrick Woods, but his father nicknamed him "Tiger" after a friend he had known from his days in the U.S. Army. Tiger took an interest in golf before he was old enough to walk. His father would hit balls into a net in their garage in Cypress, California. Tiger would watch from his highchair, squealing with joy every time his father hit the ball. Tiger would imitate his father's swing. Once Tiger could walk, Earl gave him some clubs he had shortened to Tiger's size. Now Tiger could hit the ball himself!

Tiger was a natural. Even when he was just a toddler, his swing was smooth. By age 2, he was hitting the ball so well that a local television station did a story about him. Soon after, he appeared on a national talk show, The Mike Douglas Show. He hit a few balls and putted with Bob Hope. The legend of Tiger Woods was getting started. It was clear he was a golfing **prodigy,** a player who is unusually good at a young age.

Here 12-year-old Tiger has fun as he practices putting.

→

Golf might seem like a difficult game to understand, but the basics are easy. On each hole, the golfer tries to hit the ball into the hole using as few shots, or strokes, as possible. Millions of people play golf for fun. For an **amateur** player, any score under 90 for 18 holes, or 45 for nine holes, is considered good. Tiger Woods scored a 48 for nine holes when he was just three years old!

As he grew, his game began to develop. He learned to use all of the different clubs that golfers use. But being a successful golfer was harder for Tiger than for other people. Tiger's family didn't have a lot of money, so they couldn't afford to join a private golf club where Tiger could play all the time. Tiger learned to play on public courses that weren't as nice as the fancy private ones. His parents saw how important golf was to him, and they took out loans to help pay for sending him to tournaments and lessons.

Tiger had another hurdle to overcome. He found that some people didn't like him just because of the color of his skin. When he was in first grade, some older kids tied him to a tree and threw stones at him, calling him racial names. He encountered **racism** on the golf course, too. Golf has long been a game played mostly by white people. Tiger found that many people didn't like an African American—especially one so young—playing in tournaments and winning. Tiger learned that the best way to overcome racism was to let his ability do his talking for him.

At just 16 years old, Tiger tees off on the 11th hole at the 1992 Los Angeles Open.

EARLY SUCCESS

Tiger started playing in tournaments for kids age 10 and under when he was 5 years old. Playing in local tournaments in Southern California, Tiger began winning immediately. He played in his first international event at the age of 6. It was the Optimist International Junior World tournament. He finished eighth in the field of 150 golfers from around the world, many of them five years older than he was.

Two years later, he won that tournament for the first time. It was his first victory against international competition. He would go on to win the Optimist International Junior World age-group championships six times. At the age of 14, he became the youngest golfer to win the Insurance Youth Golf Classic, another important competition. The legend of Tiger Woods was taking shape. The golf world began to realize that he was special.

Tiger reacts after dropping a birdie putt on the 15th hole at the 1993 Los Angeles Open.

→

Because Tiger's family didn't have a lot of money, he usually would arrive at tournaments on the same day they started. Other golfers would have been there for days, practicing on the course. Because of this, Tiger often didn't score as well in the first day or two of a tournament. He would still be learning how to play the course.

By the last day of a four-day tournament, however, Tiger knew the course and would rally from behind. He developed a reputation as a "finisher," someone who would come from behind to win in the end. Many times, his name wouldn't be among the leaders at the start of the last day. But by the end of the day, he was on top.

Tiger won his first national title, the U.S. Junior Amateur, in 1991 when he was just 15 years old. He was the youngest player ever to win the event. He was already ranked among the top amateur players in the country. No one had ever won the tournament more than once. Tiger won it again the next two years.

In 1994, he played in the most prestigious amateur tournament in the world, the U.S. Amateur. In this tournament, golfers play two rounds, and the players with the best scores advance to a match-play tournament. In **match play,** you play against another golfer head-to-head. Whichever golfer has the best score on a hole wins the hole. The player who wins the most holes wins the match.

Tiger celebrates after dropping a birdie putt on his way to winning his third U.S. Amateur championship in a row.

Match play was made for Tiger Woods. With his superior concentration, he was able to outthink his opponent and outplay them at the same time. This was his fourth trip to the U.S. Amateur, and he now had the confidence that he could win. In the final match, played over 36 holes, Tiger was as many as six holes behind Trip Kuehne. With nine holes to play, he trailed by three holes. It was time for Tiger to show his skills as a finisher. He charged from behind to win the tournament. He was only 18 years old, the youngest ever to win the U.S. Amateur.

Tiger won the U.S. Amateur again in 1995. All the while, Tiger was also playing golf for his college team at Stanford University. In 1996, he became just the third player ever to win the U.S. Amateur and the NCAA Championship in the same year.

TIGER THE PRO

By this time, Tiger had achieved all of his amateur goals. His amateur career was one of the best in the history of golf. He was an excellent student, but the attention he was getting was making it harder for him to stay in college. He finally turned **professional** on August 27, 1996, at the age of 20. He played in his first professional tournament, the Greater Milwaukee Open.

Playing for Stanford, Tiger chips onto the 6th green during the 1996 NCAA Men's Golf Championship.

Because Tiger had never been a pro before, he had to be invited to play in a tournament. He needed to finish among the top 125 players in money won in order to qualify for all the events the next year. He made that his goal for the eight events he was invited to in 1996—to earn enough to be able to play in all the tournaments in 1997. He went well beyond that.

Tiger finished 60th in his first tournament, then 11th in his second. In the next two tournaments he finished fifth and third. He was already 128th on the money list, needing only to pass three more players to be **exempt** in 1997. In just his fifth event, Tiger won the Las Vegas Invitational. Later, he won the Disney World/Oldsmobile Classic. In those eight events, Tiger had won more than $790,000, and had moved up to 25th on the money list. He was named PGA Tour Rookie of the Year.

MASTERS CHAMPION

There are four special tournaments on the PGA Tour called "majors": the Masters, the U.S. Open, the British Open, and the PGA Championship. The 1997 Masters was Tiger's first major tournament as a professional. Some people wondered if he would be nervous because everyone expected him to win.

Tiger reacts after hitting a hole-in-one during his first professional tournament, the 1996 Greater Milwaukee Open.

→

As usual, Tiger rose to the occasion. He not only won, but he set a new record for the tournament with his total score of 270—18 under par, for four rounds. He won by 12 strokes, which was also a record. He won a total of four PGA Tour events in 1997 and gained the Number 1 spot in the world golf rankings. At age 21, Tiger was the youngest player to reach the top spot by more than eight years!

In 1998, he won only one tournament while he was making a change in his swing. Some people thought Tiger was losing his edge because he had already earned so much money. The truth was, he was changing his game so he could be more successful in the future. It worked! In 1999, Tiger won eight tournaments, including his second major, the PGA Championship. His earnings total of more than $6.6 million was $3 million more than the next-highest player.

Tiger won the last four tournaments in which he played in 1999, the longest such streak in 46 years. Then, he won his first two tournaments of the 2000 season!

TIGER TODAY

Today, Tiger is the best golfer in the world. He has won 18 tournaments already, and he's only 24 years old. Off the course, Tiger started the Tiger Woods Foundation, which gives minorities a better chance to play golf. Tiger's father runs the foundation. And whenever there is a golf tournament in which he plays, you can expect to see his name on the leaderboard!

Grass flies as Tiger sends a ball down the fairway at the 2000 Nissan Open.

December 30, 1975	Eldrick "Tiger" Woods is born.
1983	Tiger wins the Optimist International Junior World, the first of six times he wins this tournament.
1991	Tiger becomes the youngest player to win the U.S. Junior Amateur Championship.
1992	Tiger becomes the first player to win the U.S. Junior Amateur twice.
1993	Tiger wins the U.S. Junior Amateur for the third time. He accepts a scholarship to Stanford University.
1994	Tiger becomes the youngest winner of the U.S. Amateur.
1996	Tiger becomes the first player to win three straight U.S. Amateur championships. He becomes the third player to win a NCAA Championship and a U.S. Amateur in the same year. He wins two different College Player of the Year awards and is named First-Team All-American. He joins the PGA Tour, wins two of the eight tournaments in which he plays on the Tour, and is named PGA Tour Rookie of the Year.
1997	Tiger wins the Masters and three other PGA Tour events. He is the Tour's leading money winner ($2,440,832) and is named PGA Tour Player of the Year. He achieves the world Number 1 ranking faster than any other player in history.
1998	Tiger wins one PGA Tour event and two other events.
1999	Tiger wins eight PGA Tour events, including the PGA Championship. He is named PGA Tour Player of the Year and sets a Tour earnings record with more than $6.6 million.

Tiger helps a young golfer with his swing during a golf clinic in Dallas.

GLOSSARY

amateur (AM–uh–cher)
A person who does not get paid to participate in an activity is an amateur. Tiger had one of the best amateur golf careers in history.

course (CORSS)
A group of 18 golf holes is called a golf course. Tiger had to learn about golf courses while he was playing them because he couldn't come to tournaments early to practice.

exempt (egg–ZEMPT)
A player who is eligible to play in all PGA Tour events in a given year is called exempt. Tiger became exempt after just eight events in 1996.

match play (MATCH PLAY)
In match play, two golfers play against each other to see who wins the most holes. Tiger is one of the best match-play golfers ever.

prodigy (PRAH–dih–jee)
A person who is unusually good at something at a young age is called a prodigy. Tiger was a golf prodigy.

professional (proh–FEH–shun–ull)
A professional is someone who is paid for his or her work. Tiger became a professional after winning his third straight U.S. Amateur.

racism (RAY–sih–zem)
A belief that some races of people are better than others is called racism. Tiger had to overcome racism, both on the golf course and off.

tournament (TOOR–nuh–ment)
A sporting competition that includes many competitors is called a tournament. Tiger has won many golf tournaments.

INDEX